The Police Station

Sue Barraclough

Photographs by Chris Fairclough

FRANKLIN WATTS
LONDON • SYDNEY

Contents

The police station

A police station is a building where police officers are based. Police officers work together to prevent and solve **crimes**, and to keep people safe.

This police station has a big garage and parking for police vehicles, so officers can respond quickly to any **emergency**.

Some officers spend most of their time away from the police station on **patrol**.

Teams of office staff (below) work at the station, alongside the police officers.

The team

Police officers work in teams or units with different jobs to do. Kevin is a chief superintendent. As a **manager**, he makes decisions about how the police station is run, and the jobs that other officers do each day.

Stuart is a sergeant. He is in charge of the **response team**. He keeps track of the team, and makes sure they are in the right place when they are needed.

Clare (right) is a police community support officer, or PCSO. She goes out on street patrols. She lets people know she is there to help.

Diane (left) is a scene of crime officer, or SOCO. She goes to places where crimes have happened to gather **evidence**.

Canteen

In the canteen, busy officers and other staff can relax with hot food and drinks.

Starting a shift

Police officers work **shifts**. This means that as one team finishes work, another one starts. Officers put on their **uniforms** before they start work.

Hot desking

In some offices, there is a hot desk system. This means that the officers don't have their own desks. There are a number of desks set up with a computer and other **equipment**, and each officer just goes to a desk that is free when they start their shift.

At the start of each shift, there is a **briefing**. The officers are given maps, photos and other information to help them carry out their tasks.

At the front desk

The front desk and **reception** area are often busy because visitors arrive here when they come to the building.

There is also a machine which visitors can use to get information.

Malcolm works on the front desk. He spends most of his time giving help and advice to visitors, and answering questions on the phone.

'I am often the first person people see when they arrive. I try to be as helpful as possible.'
Malcolm, front desk officer

People come in to the police station to report crimes and to tell the police about things they have lost.

The CCTV room

Karen works at the control desk in the closed-circuit TV (**CCTV**) room. From her desk Karen can see screens which show views of the streets in the local area.

Karen sees someone snatch a handbag in a busy street. She uses her radio to pass a message to a police officer nearby.

Karen makes sure she keeps a video tape of what happened. The tape can be used as evidence in **court**.

The mobile CCTV van

There is also a **mobile** CCTV van that can be used to film people and places.

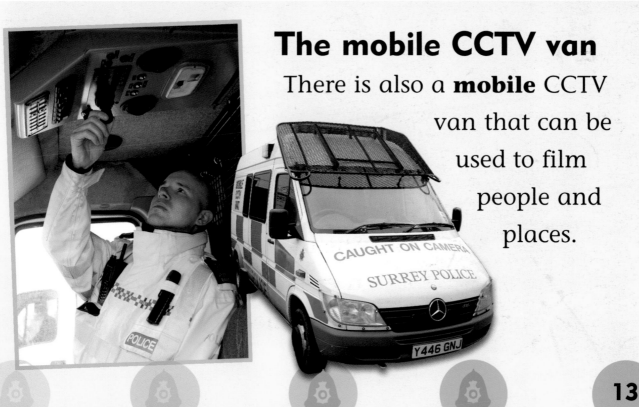

Vehicles and equipment

Police cars are brightly coloured and have lights and sirens to warn other road users that they are driving fast to an emergency.

Each car has equipment in the boot. There are cones and lights to use at traffic accidents, and a **first-aid kit**.

Police cars have **satellite navigation** to help the officers find their way quickly to an incident.

Working together

The police work closely with the ambulance and fire services at a road traffic accident. A big team work together to get drivers out of the vehicles and take injured people to a hospital.

Then the police work out how the accident happened and make a report.

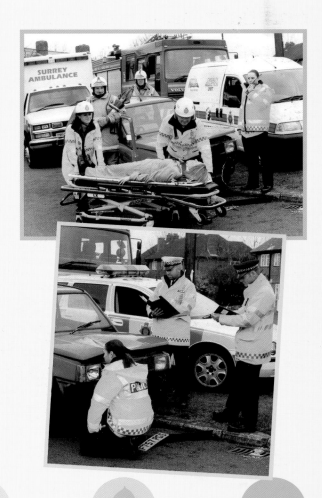

Response teams

The response team is on **standby** to go out to emergencies. The team has a big board that shows which police vehicles have been called out from the police station.

When a call comes in from the **call handling centre**, the response team sends a car to deal with the emergency.

While an officer is away from the station he keeps in touch with the rest of his team on his radio.

Emergency calls

The police call handling centre is where operators answer all 999 calls, and pass them to the nearest police station. One centre covers a number of police stations.

Scene of crime officer

Diane is a scene of crime officer, or SOCO. She goes to a place where a crime has happened to collect evidence.

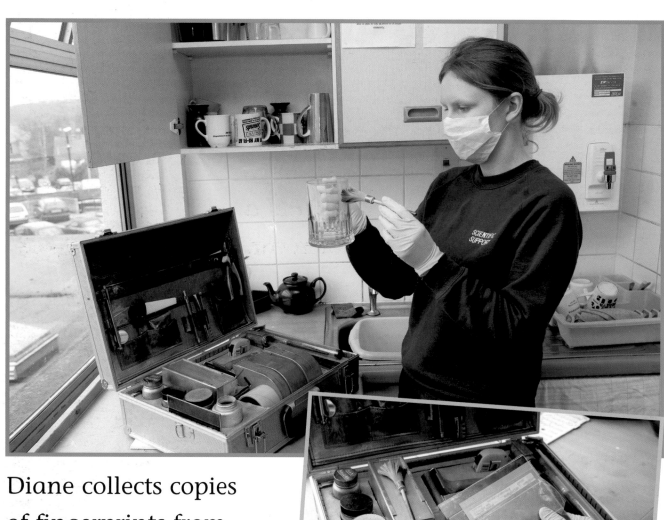

Diane collects copies of fingerprints from any objects that may have been touched by a **burglar**.

Diane wears a special suit for serious crimes. The suit covers her whole body because the scene of the crime must be kept clean and clear while evidence is gathered.

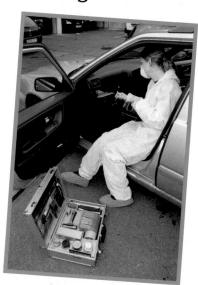

Here, Diane is taking a **swab** in a stolen car.

Gathering evidence

Each person has a unique set of fingerprints so prints can be very important evidence. This print is labelled and sent off for safekeeping.

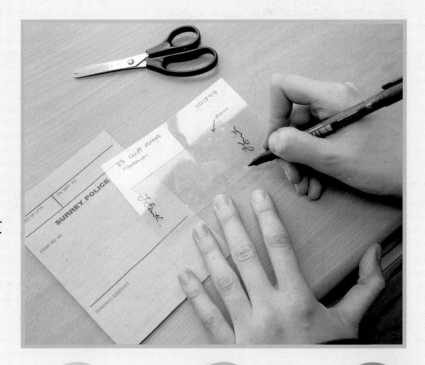

Detective work

Dene is a detective, which means he **investigates** crimes. Here he is typing up some of his notes from a murder investigation.

Dene works with uniformed officers. Here, he is talking about a **case** with Ebbe.

Dene also goes out and about to gather evidence.

Here, Dene talks to a **witness** about a **burglary**.

'I deal with different crimes to try to find out who did them. I talk to witnesses and work with other officers to share information.'
Dene, detective

Court cases

Once all the evidence is gathered a case goes to court. A detective often goes to the **trial**. Dene has just finished showing the evidence he had gathered to a **judge**.

Under arrest

Dene has **arrested** a man for burglary and brought him to the police station.

The **suspect** is **interviewed** by Dene, and everything is recorded.

The suspect's fingerprints are **scanned**. The fingerprints will be checked against prints collected at the scene of the crime.

The suspect is checked in by the desk sergeant.

Then a **custody officer** escorts the suspect to one of the **cells**.

Taking fingerprints

This is the old fashioned way of taking fingerprints. This method is sometimes still used when the fingerprinting machine is not working.

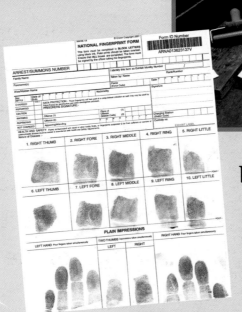

Each finger is inked on an inkpad, and pressed firmly on the paper.

Neighbourhood teams

The neighbourhood teams go out on patrol. Trevor and Clare go out on patrol every day to make sure all is well.

'Talking to local people is an important part of our job.'
Clare, PCSO

Trevor is reporting some new graffiti that will need to be removed.

Trevor and Clare know the area very well. Clare chats about parking problems, while Trevor checks that an empty shop is locked up properly.

Neighbourhood Watch

Neighbourhood Watch is a charity. It helps set up local groups of people to watch over the area. They work with police to make their neighbourhood safer and to help prevent crimes.

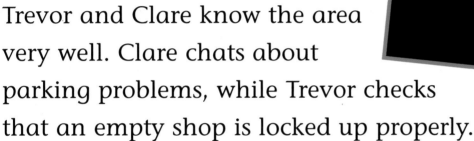

Special units

Some officers are trained to work in a Police Special Unit, or PSU. PSUs deal with incidents such as trouble at football matches or other crowded events.

Kelly puts on this PSU uniform to protect her if the unit is called to an incident such as a fight between rival fans at a football match.

'It gets really hot if I have to wear the PSU gear for a long time.'
Kelly, police constable

Other units

This officer is a police dog handler. Dogs are often called in to follow a **scent**, because they have such a good sense of smell. Sometimes they are used to help find missing people.

The police sometimes use helicopters for police work. These letters and numbers on top of police vehicles mean they can be identified from above. This helps the helicopter pilot to keep in touch with the officers in the van.

At the end of a shift

In the response office, police constable Cheryl is typing up a report at the end of her shift.

Cheryl hangs her car keys on the board, so the officer who takes over can find them easily.

Police constable Megan has changed out of uniform, and it's time to go home.

Staff are already arriving for the next shift. The front desk staff make sure they tell the new team about anything important that has happened.

# Glossary

arrested a person is arrested if the police think he or she has broken a law.

briefing a meeting to give people information to help them do their jobs.

burglar a person who breaks in and steals things from people's homes.

burglary when someone breaks in to people's homes and steals things.

call handling centre a place where 999 emergency calls are received.

case a crime that is being investigated by the police.

CCTV closed-circuit television is a camera that records what happens in a certain place.

cells small rooms where suspects are locked in.

court a building where trials take place.

crimes doing things that are against the law.

custody officer an officer who looks after suspects in the cells.

emergency something that needs urgent action.

equipment things you need to do a task.

evidence something that will prove that a fact is true.

first-aid kit box containing medicines for use in an emergency.

interviewed asked someone questions.

investigates searches for facts and information.

judge a person who decides if someone has done a crime.

manager someone who is in charge of a place of work.

mobile something that can be moved easily.

patrol to go out to check that all is well in a certain area.

reception a place in a building to welcome visitors.

response team a team of police officers.

satellite navigation a machine that helps you find your way around.

scanned to take a picture of something.

scent a smell left by a person or animal.

shift a period of hours that people work.

standby to be ready for action.

suspect someone who may have done something wrong (against the law).

swab a sample of a substance.

trial a meeting to decide if someone is guilty of a crime.

uniforms clothes that show the job that you do.

witness a person who has seen something happen.

Further information

Websites

www.surrey.police.uk The police station featured in this book is part of the Surrey police. Visit this website to find out more.

www.met.police.uk Website of London's Metropolitan Police. It includes a 'Young People' section.

www.neighbourhoodwatch.net Facts, news and useful information on keeping safe.

Books

Police Officer (When I'm at Work), Sue Barraclough, Franklin Watts, 2005.

The Police (People Who Help Us), Clare Oliver, Franklin Watts, 2002.

Every effort has been made by the Packagers and Publishers to ensure that these websites contain no inappropriate or offensive material. However, because of the nature of the Internet, it is not possible to guarantee that the contents of these sites will not be altered. We strongly advise that Internet access is supervised by a responsible adult.

 Index